THE
ANCIENT EGYPTIANS
Life in the Nile Valley

BY VIVIANE KOENIG

Illustrations by Véronique Ageorges
Translated by Mary Kae LaRose

PEOPLES OF THE PAST

The Millbrook Press
Brookfield, Connecticut

Library of Congress Cataloging-in-Publication Data
Koenig, Viviane.
[Au bord du Nil. English]
The ancient Egyptians: life in the Nile valley / by Viviane Koenig;
illustrations by Véronique Ageorges; translated by Mary Kae LaRose.
p. cm.—(Peoples of the past)
Translation of: Au bord du Nil.
Includes bibliographical references and index.
Summary: Details the daily lives of the ancient Egyptians in the Nile Valley,
describing their work, clothing, schools, social, economic, and religious traditions.
ISBN 1-56294-161-5
1. Egypt—Civilization—To 332 B.C.—Juvenile literature.
[1. Egypt—Civilization—To 332 B.C.] I. Ageorges, Véronique, ill.
II. Title. III. Series: Peoples of the past (Brookfield, Conn.)
DT61.K6413 1992
932—dc20   91-25772 CIP AC

First published in the United States by
The Millbrook Press Inc.
2 Old New Milford Road, Brookfield, Connecticut 06804

Translation copyright © 1992 by The Millbrook Press
Copyright © 1990 by Editions Nathan, Paris

Originally published as Au bord du Nil, les Égyptiens
(Peuples du passé series), Editions Nathan, Paris

CONTENTS

INTRODUCTION

This book is about people who lived in the Nile River valley in Egypt thousands of years ago. Much food was grown in the fertile soil of the valley, and many animals grazed there. Boats came and went, carrying goods and people up and down the mighty river. It is easy to understand why the ancient Egyptians thought of their river as a god. The Nile waters brought life to the people, and they, in turn, created one of the first and most long lasting civilizations in history.

This culture began to form about five thousand years ago and lasted for more than two thousand years. It's hard to imagine that boys and girls, men and women who lived so long ago experienced many of the same things we do today. They played games, discussed the latest fashions, wrote down their thoughts, sang and played music, grew tired at the end of a long workday, and looked forward to a good meal. They were also curious about their world. They wondered where it came from, why the sun rose in the morning and the stars filled the sky at night, and what would happen to them when they died.

It has only been in the last few hundred years that archaeologists have dug into the earth to uncover what is left of the Egyptians' towns, temples, and tombs. We have learned a lot about these ancient people by studying their jewelry, writing, paintings, sculpture, and architecture. Through the traces they left behind, they talk to us, telling us who they were, what they dreamed of doing, and how much they accomplished in their lifetime.

TIME TABLE

With the union of Upper and Lower Egypt, Egyptian civilization begins, around 3100 B.C.
Government, science, architecture, and writing are born.

OLD KINGDOM 2780–2280 B.C.
The step pyramid of King Djoser is the first large stone building in the world.
King Khufu's Great Pyramid at Giza is built, the world's largest building until modern times.
People pray to the sun god Re, and the first religious words are written on the walls of royal tombs.

FIRST INTERMEDIATE PERIOD 2280–2050 B.C.
The central government breaks down, and regional governors divide the land among themselves.
Much writing comes from this period.
King Mentuhotep reunites the country and moves the capital from Memphis to Thebes.

MIDDLE KINGDOM 2050–1786 B.C.
The government becomes strong under the rule of King Amenemhet I.

SECOND INTERMEDIATE PERIOD 1786–1570 B.C.
Western Asiatic groups gain control of Egypt.
Weapons, horses, and chariots are introduced.

NEW KINGDOM (EMPIRE PERIOD) 1570–1085 B.C.
Princes drive out foreign rulers and expand the Egyptian Empire into Asia and Africa. Its golden age begins.

The capital is again in Memphis. The powerful rulers of this period are Hatshepsut, Amenhotep III and Tiy, Akhenaton and Nefertiti, Tutankhamen and Ankhesenamen.

Great temples are built throughout the country, particularly at Thebes (at Luxor and Karnak). Royalty is buried in the Valley of the Kings.

THIRD INTERMEDIATE PERIOD (POST EMPIRE) 1085–663 B.C.

The kings weaken, and Egypt is no longer a world power.

Civil war and foreign invaders tear Egypt apart.

THE SAÏTE PERIOD 663–525 B.C.

People from other countries, including the Greeks, settle in Egypt.

THE PERSIAN CONQUEST 525–405 B.C.

The Persians invade and rule Egypt from 525 B.C. to 404 B.C., when they are pushed out.

ALEXANDER THE GREAT conquers Egypt in 332 B.C.

PTOLEMAIC PERIOD 323–30 B.C.

When Alexander dies, General Ptolemy takes the title of king and forms the dynasty of the Ptolemies. In the third century B.C., Alexandria becomes the new capital and the home of the greatest library of the ancient world. In 37 B.C., Queen Cleopatra VII of the Ptolemies marries Mark Antony, a co-ruler of Rome. In the Battle of Actium, they lose to Octavian, another co–ruler of Rome. Cleopatra and Antony commit suicide in 30 B.C., and Egypt becomes part of the Roman Empire. Two thousand years will pass before the next native–born Egyptian will rule the land.

THE NILE, SOURCE OF LIFE

The Nile River, born in the heart of Africa, was the source of life in ancient Egypt. After flowing northward across several thousand miles of desert, its waters spilled over into many giant, crashing waterfalls and dangerous rapids called cataracts. These swiftly running waters boomed and roared. Suddenly, at the Nile delta, the river calmed down. It split into many small branches that flowed gently toward the Mediterranean Sea.

Every summer the Nile rose and flooded the vast river valley. It receded in the fall, leaving behind a thin, rich layer of silt, a gift to the workers who cultivated its freshly fertilized soil.

All these elements were gods to the ancient Egyptians. Year after year, it was the river god who brought them life by flooding the land with the gushing waters of the Nile.

Its waters carried something other than fish and silt, however. Crocodiles lived there, too. They hid in the papyrus thickets and lounged around on sandbanks, ready to plunge into

THE RIVER GOD

The ancient Egyptians believed that the earth was shaped like a big fat pancake. In the center of the cake flowed the Nile, and around the flat center stretched the wide ocean known as the Great Circle. They believed that the sky above was as flat as the earth. Four poles held it up, allowing air to flow between the earth and the sky.

Why the Nile?

The ancient Egyptians called their river Hapy. The name Nile comes from the Greek word Neilos, whose origin remains uncertain.

the water to snap up a fish or to gobble up a hapless swimmer or fisherman.

Hippopotamus herds might appear just as suddenly as crocodiles. These enormous animals ate nothing but grass, but because they could devour an entire field of wheat, barley, or flax within minutes, the ancients were as afraid of them as they were of crocodiles.

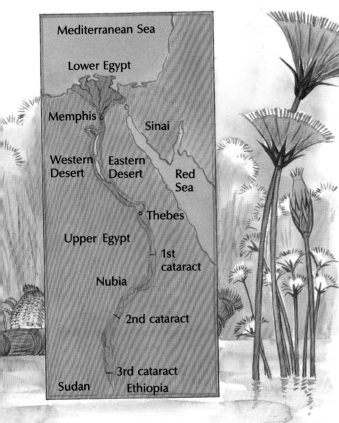

Mediterranean Sea

Lower Egypt

Memphis

Sinai

Western Desert

Eastern Desert

Red Sea

Thebes

Upper Egypt

1st cataract

Nubia

2nd cataract

3rd cataract

Sudan

Ethiopia

TRAVEL ON THE NILE

In ancient times, the Nile was the fastest way to travel through the land. Every day, by dawn, many different kinds of boats began to pass each other on the river. Small skiffs made from bundles of papyrus stalks hugged the riverbanks and slipped easily through the marshes and channels.

Wooden boats used sails to travel with the wind, which usually came from the north.

But when they headed downstream (or north), men had to use paddles or long poles, which they dug into the banks or the muddy bed of the shallow waters, to move their craft swiftly forward.

Because traffic was heavy on the river, the people steering their light skiffs had to be careful not to bump into the heavy wooden boats owned by the pharaoh, the king of Egypt.

Only the pharaoh, or perhaps the very wealthy, owned large wooden boats (measuring more than 100 feet, or 30 meters, long) because the lack of tall trees in Egypt made wood very expensive. Cedar had to be imported from Lebanon on the eastern coast of the Mediterranean. Workers cut it into sturdy planks, which boat builders turned into pleasure craft to carry people, or barges and cargo boats to transport goods along the river.

Cargo boats might carry baskets, earthenware jars, enormous blocks of granite, cattle, or food supplies. Luxurious pleasure craft had cabins to protect the passengers from the searing rays of the sun. Teams of men pulled on many sets of oars to propel these large boats. Sometimes, when the wind died out, men had to tow the boats along the river with long ropes from the banks.

THE BLACK LAND

The black color of the earth surrounding the Nile led the Egyptians to call their valley Kemet, or the Black Land. They were grateful for its fertile soil and proud to call this valley their home. And they were right to feel thankful, for it was due to these waters that the

amazing civilization in Egypt developed so early and lasted as long as it did.

But life in the valley was not easy. When the floodwaters subsided, peasants set to work on the land, breaking up lumps of earth, planting seeds, and irrigating day after day. Later, they brought in the harvest, transported the crops, and threshed the grain.

The lives of the fishermen were just as exhausting. They set off early in the morning in their flimsy papyrus skiffs. Chameleons (a type of lizard), wildcats, and thousands of colorfully plumed birds hid on the banks. Once in a while a hippopotamus upset a boat; crocodiles screamed and birds chattered and flew away. The skilled fisherman managed to right his craft and continue on through the marsh, catching fish and wild ducks to trade for other food and supplies in the village.

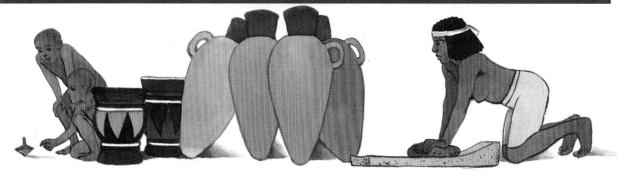

Egyptians relied on song and laughter to help them forget the fatigue and troubles of the day. On holidays, they loved to play games, sing songs, and tell stories over a glass of beer or wine. For a short while, they forgot the heat, hard work, heavy taxes, sickness, and the death of loved ones. They laughed at themselves and even made jokes about their gods and their pharaoh.

THE RED LAND

The Nile River valley has always been protected by well-defined, natural borders. To the south are the first unnavigable cataracts of the Nile; and to the north, the delta marshes spread into the sea.

To the east and west of the Nile Valley stretch large expanses of desert, which the Egyptians called Deshret, or the Red Land. Even though more than ninety percent of modern Egypt lies here, few people have made their homes on these barren plateaus of rolling sand. Only those who knew the desert well dared to travel over its blistering landscape.

How They Made Beer

They ground barley into flour and kneaded it into small round loaves.

When the dough was half-baked, they took it from the oven and mixed it with sweetened water in earthenware jugs. When the mixture had fermented, they filtered it and poured the clear liquid beer into jugs.

Laughing at Yourself

"A scribe," wrote a scribe, "has never moved an inch, and hasn't run since the day he was born. He can't bear the sight of men at work because he knows nothing about it."

And yet, these deserts served an important purpose. In a sense, they made an island of the Nile River valley, protecting it from outside influences and so allowing its unique culture to grow.

The pharaohs added to these natural boundaries by securing their kingdom from invaders with heavily guarded fortresses. Soldiers, policemen, and customs officers kept track of who came and left the country.

The border patrol made long surveillance rounds accompanied by specially trained dogs. The dogs' keen sense of smell led them to thieves escaping with their booty, peasants who were fleeing the country because they

couldn't pay their taxes, runaway slaves, and foreigners who, attracted by Egypt's wealth, wanted to settle there.

The Egyptian people were often frightened to leave their green valley. Beyond it lay the Red Land, whose rough sand and stones made it hard to walk on the barren soil. Small footpaths snaked through dried-out valleys and disappeared into the vast desert horizon.

Even after venturing deep into the desert, a traveler was never really alone. Flies buzzed around, and wild dogs barked constantly. The traveler might throw stones at them to chase them away, but stones were no protection against the lions, hyenas, and cheetahs that stalked the desert sands. Deadly horned vipers hid under rocks, and lethal scorpions skittered along the ground.

To the Egyptians the suffocating heat and

terrifying creatures of the Red Land belonged to the god Seth, who for centuries had been absolute master of the desolate Red Land. He, like many Egyptian deities, or gods, was part human and part animal. He was the god of storms and of chaos.

There is a story about how he was chosen to rule the Red Land. The court of Egyptian gods decided a case involving two opposing deities. The case had been dragging on for eighty years, and the problem had grown serious. Who was to succeed the god Osiris, Egypt's wise king—his brother Seth or his son Horus?

After many bitter discussions and turns of events, Horus finally defeated his uncle Seth in a bloody hand-to-hand combat. He took the Egyptian throne and has been ruling over

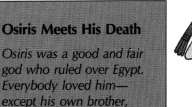

Osiris Meets His Death

Osiris was a good and fair god who ruled over Egypt. Everybody loved him—except his own brother, Seth. One day, overcome by jealousy, Seth tricked Osiris, killed him, and took his throne.

Osiris

the Nile Valley ever since. As a consolation prize, Seth was given the Egyptian desert.

Even though the ancient Egyptians didn't like the desert where Seth lorded over the dangerous animals, this was where they buried their dead. They had no choice. In the fertile, green valley, even the smallest plots of land were cultivated to feed the living.

The God of the Dead

Isis, Osiris's widow, went in search of her husband's body. Her sorrow so moved the gods that they brought Osiris back to life and let him rule over the kingdom of the dead. The couple gave birth to a child they named Horus, who later took the throne back from Seth, his father's murderer.

Horus

What Seth Looked Like

Seth was the god of the desert and of storms. When Seth howled in the sky, thunder crashed and the earth shook. The very sight of him was quite terrifying. He had red eyes, a bizarre bestial head with rectangular ears, and a drooping snout.

Seth

DAILY LIFE IN THE VALLEY

Ancient Egyptians, just like those of to-day, tended to have black hair and dark eyes, and their skin was naturally bronzed. Because of the warm weather, they dressed lightly. The cloth they used for almost all of their garments was linen, spun from the flax grown in the fields and then woven on looms. The linen of the pharaohs and wealthy people was very finely woven, but the workers wore garments of a more durable, coarse material or soft leather.

Male peasants wore simple loincloths, which hung from their waist to their knees. Sometimes, they didn't wear anything at all. On the other hand, men in the upper classes had many different styles of skirts or kilts that varied according to the fashion of the time. Some of these fastened on the side, and others knotted in the middle. They might be baggy or pleated, and some even hung to the ankles. But for peasants and gods, styles never changed.

Both country women and goddesses wore simple, tight-fitting dresses that came up to their chests and were held up by shoulder straps. Children's fashions, too, never varied. They were as simple as they could be—little Egyptians wore nothing at all!

Rich, fashionable Egyptian ladies added transparent shawls, flower headdresses, beaded collars, and sparkling jewelry to

their basic outfit. Gold was mined in the Eastern Desert and beaten and shaped into many different types of bracelets, ear ornaments, rings, belts, necklaces, and head-

A Love Poem

"One alone is my beloved more gracious than all other women. . . .
shining, precious, white of skin, lovely of eyes when gazing. Sweet her lips when speaking, she has no excess of words. Long of neck, white of breast, her hair true lapis lazuli."

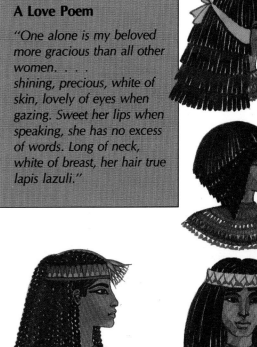

pieces. Semiprecious stones—carnelian, feldspar, and amethyst—came from the desert. And turquoise and lapis lazuli were imported from the Sinai peninsula and from as far away as Afghanistan.

Egyptians, as a rule, were an extremely fashion-conscious people. They loved to adorn themselves and had a highly developed sense of personal beauty.

Both men and women wore eye makeup, not only because they liked how it looked, but out of necessity. The desert's beating sun and swarming flies caused eye infections. In the spring, conditions grew worse when a hot wind blew across the desert, bringing sand and dust. It scratched the eyes and made it hard to breathe in the open air.

What Were Their Sandals Like?

The sandals worn by the upper classes were often pointed and turned up at the end. They were made of papyrus stalks, woven palm leaves, or leather. Sandals of artists and artisans appear to have been nothing more than soles and a few straps.

To protect their eyes against irritation, Egyptians used a black lead ore called galena, which they ground into a powder in a little mortar dish. They then mixed this black powder with fat or cream and stored it in a pretty stone pot. They applied the cream with a cosmetic spoon. It was an excellent medication. Unfortunately though, because it was very expensive, its soothing effects were felt only by those who could afford it.

Egyptians often shaved their heads to protect themselves from fleas and lice. But, as soon as their heads were shaven clean and the problem was solved, their hair began to grow back. Men had bushy hairstyles that could be either long or short, depending on what was in style. Women preferred to have hair long, which they

wore either loose or braided or tied back with headbands and decorated with flowers or jewels.

Wealthy Egyptians often treated themselves to pretty braided wigs that protected them from the sun. They perfumed their wigs and twisted them into fancy curls with special tongs. Children's hairstyles, like their clothing, never changed: Their hair was simply shaved off. A side lock was often left, though, to hang down several inches from one side of their head.

CITY DWELLERS

Egyptians lived in cramped conditions. Because of the yearly spring floods, they built their towns and cities on small hills. When the Nile overflowed its banks, only clusters

of huts would rise above the water's surface. From a distance they looked as though they had been built on an island.

A grid of narrow streets separated the modest houses, which were made of brick and stone. Each house had a low arched doorway, a few small windows closed by wooden shutters, a dirt floor, and a cool place to store food. The entire family might live in one or two small rooms, but in the summer they often spent time chatting and sleeping on the terraced rooftop, where they could take advantage of the cool evening air.

A typical luxurious house was shaded by palm trees and sycamores and hidden from view by a big wall. It was spacious and made of brick coated over with plaster. A large entrance hall led to many bedrooms. There were also kitchens, servants' quarters, store-

rooms, cellars, and stables spread throughout the garden, beneath the house, and on the terrace.

Residents of such a house would stroll in the garden or, seated by the pool, watch fish weave in and out among the water lilies and lotus leaves. They were fascinated by frogs and dragonflies. And here, in their backyard, they had their own piece of nature to explore. But as night fell, the sound of mosquitoes filled the air, and people tended to head for the protection of the house.

Mosquitoes were not the only enemy of the Egyptians, however. The sun was also a problem. There were days when going outside felt like stepping into a massive scorching oven. The terrace faced north to catch the coolest breezes, as did the windows, which were also often covered with grillwork that let in as little dust and light as possible. Vents were built into the walls to circulate cool air inside the house.

Recipe for Bricks

Take some silt from the banks of the Nile. Mix it with water and a bit of finely chopped straw. Place the mixture in a rectangular wooden mold. Pack it down. Remove the mold and let the block dry in the sun for several hours.

Did They Have Toilets?

Toilets were rare, but they did exist. Small seats made from stone or wood were placed on top of low walls. Stools with a hole carved in the middle were also used. In both cases, a baked clay container filled with sand was placed beneath the hole.

Because Egyptian houses were exposed to the strong rays of the sun and the damaging floodwaters of the Nile, they tended to fall apart very quickly. Mud flaked off, bricks eroded, and walls cracked and crumbled. But houses were rebuilt almost as fast as they fell down. The debris was cleared away, and new homes were raised on the old stone foundations. This explains why, over the course of centuries, towns and cities gradually came to sit higher above the valley floor.

LIVING OFF THE LAND

The ancients loved their land, which they believed to embody the great god Geb. They imagined Geb as a man whose skin was as green as the grass that grew on his back.

Crops were abundant. A Greek traveler wrote, "Once the fields were planted, Egyptian peasants had nothing to do except wait for harvest time." Alas, reality was altogether different.

Even when the Nile covered the fields, the peasants who worked the land had no time to rest. They had to make new tools and repair the old ones. They needed hoes and plows made of wood, pickaxes for turning up the earth, baskets and cloth bags to carry grain, and earthenware jugs to carry water to the fields. Their work never stopped. If there was a lull in the preparations for planting, they might be enlisted to work on one of the pharaoh's large construction projects.

As soon as the Nile receded, peasants began repairing the damage caused by the floods. They reinforced riverbanks and cleared blocked canals. Then they had to use a team of oxen—one or two would be enough to pull a plow. They would also need a few

donkeys to carry the heavy bags of seed; the peasants walked alongside the donkeys, sowing the muddy fields.

The sun was so hot that the peasants had to irrigate their fields every day. They maintained countless little canals that crisscrossed the fields, allowing the waters of the Nile to nourish the plants.

At the end of the day, in spite of their exhaustion, the workers often sat in the relative coolness of their terraces or front steps as they checked their tools and spliced together ropes for the next day's work.

And they would share a meal, which always included bread. Egyptians baked at least forty different kinds, using different combinations of flour kneaded into round, cone-

Long Live The Family!

Egyptian families often included grandparents, parents, and several children. Families might also take in an unmarried aunt or an orphaned cousin. Egyptian families were warm and loving. A wise man once advised, "Love your wife with passion. Feed her, clothe her, and make her happy for as long as you live."

shaped, or oval loaves. Sometimes they added honey, milk, and eggs to sweeten its taste. Their bread came from the barley and wheat that they grew in their fields. The grain was stored in granaries in their homes until it was time to grind it into flour for bread or beer.

A typical meal for a peasant might be boiled or roasted meat or poultry; assorted vegetables and fruits, particularly figs and grapes; a slice of bread; and some beer. From time to time, depending on the day's catch, their meals would also include fish.

Tax Time

The king's messengers crisscrossed the countryside collecting taxes owed to the pharaoh. They made three visits a year accompanied by a scribe, an official writer for the king. The first time, shortly after the Nile waters had subsided, they measured the fields and wrote down the names of the peasants in charge of cultivating them. Several weeks later, they returned to inspect the young sprouts of wheat, flax, and barley. By fore-

casting the upcoming harvest, they calculated the taxes owed. On their third visit, just as the peasants were bringing in the harvest, they collected the king's share.

Since money didn't exist yet, Egyptians paid their taxes with goods, such as sacks of grain. The scribe and his assistants counted the sacks and checked on their papyrus scrolls to make sure that the quantities corresponded to their calculations. Once everything was in order, they carried away a good part of the harvest. Peasants often argued with the tax collectors, but the law of the land was strictly enforced.

A Horrible Punishment

An old Egyptian scribe tells how taxes were levied. "Accompanied by guards armed with clubs and palm tree branches, the scribe went to collect harvest taxes. 'Give us the grain,' they said, but there wasn't any. The guards beat the peasant, tied him up, and threw him into the well. His wife was thrown in after him, and his children were chained up. His neighbors did nothing to help."

The scribe may have exaggerated a bit, but how far was he from the truth?

Who Dared to Cheat?

"Anybody caught altering the boundaries of the land belonging to the pharaoh's temple will be punished by law. His ears will be cut off, and he will become a worker in the temple."

The Egyptians thought twice before trying to cheat the king by moving the boundary stones in their fields.

Natural Disasters

Aside from tax day, peasants worried about the whims of nature, which they often attributed to the ill wishes of the gods. Some years, birds pecked away the seeds they had planted. Or, hippopotamuses might climb from the river to graze on the banks, and work their way to the young wheat and corn maturing in the fields. Sometimes, clouds of grasshoppers appeared and devoured the entire harvest in minutes.

Peasants were also afraid of famine caused by too much or too little flooding. When this happened, the palace or temples came to

Could They Run Away?

When a peasant couldn't pay his taxes, he sometimes fled to the desert. Often, though, the peasant's entire family would be taken hostage by the police and put in prison.

their aid by distributing emergency portions of grain to the hungry people.

Peasants had to work with hoes and pickaxes and put up with taxes, hippos, grasshoppers, snakes, birds, and bad floods. Their diet of bread, meat and fish, vegetables, and beer, combined with constant physical labor, kept them slim. They looked at those who grew fat eating large quantities of rich food as among the privileged. Only the officials and scribes had plump, round tummies and double chins. Nothing could be more elegant! The peasant who saw a plump person go by was jealous of the pleasant, comfortable life of the wealthy.

HUNTING, FISHING, AND TENDING LIVESTOCK

Egyptians lived surrounded by many different kinds of animals. Some of those they hunted were the gazelle; the wild goat, ox, and sheep; the hare; and the porcupine. Every now and then a fisherman would have the good luck of catching a goose or a wild duck. He would then be able to offer his family the treat of roasted fowl at dinnertime.

However, hunting was also a sport enjoyed by many, including kings and their royal followers. A nobleman might fill a papyrus skiff with his servants, family members, and his hunting dogs. The prince would heave a special throw stick at a covey of flying ducks, taking pleasure in his sport. His men would place nets among the papyrus thickets and then close them in a flash to trap a whole covey of birds at once. Sometimes the nobleman and his companions carried spears and tried to kill hippopotamuses and crocodiles.

Once in a while, a nobleman would go off into the desert to hunt. Despite the company of his servants, he advanced with caution. Men always hunted in a group armed with bows and arrows, ropes, and daggers.

They dug well-camouflaged ditches in which to hide. The archer had to have a good aim to catch a lion or a hyena. Such sport could prove deadly.

The pharaoh himself hunted wild animals in the desert, often from a horse-driven chariot. For the king, this was a symbolic gesture. By doing away with fearsome animals, he was using his magic powers to fight and kill off the enemies of his kingdom. In this way,

he protected his people and proved that he was still young, strong, and powerful.

Egyptian hunting weapons were simple and only as good as the hunters who used them. Most often, hunters shot arrows with powerful bows or threw boomerangs to wound their prey. Once the animal was down, they moved in for the kill with daggers or spears. These weapons were made out of wood, bronze, and copper.

Fishermen

Fishermen lived in cabins near the marshes. Teams of these men were supervised by a civil servant armed with a long stick. At dawn, the group began to move slowly through the deep water, fishing with spears or placing traps and nets and dragging them back out again. Several men worked side by side, and if they were quick they caught many fish.

Some days, teams of fishermen rode in two papyrus skiffs, dragging a large net between them. Others, seated on chairs, cast lines with dangling hooks into the river.

Eels, mullet, carp, perch, and big-toothed catfish were snared from the Nile. Egyptians did a lot of fishing and loved to eat their catch grilled, fresh, salted, or dried.

Shepherds

Shepherds lived in sheds made of reeds in the prairies bordering the Nile marshlands.

After trying unsuccessfully to raise various kinds of desert livestock, such as gazelles, antelopes, and even hyenas, Egyptian shepherds took to raising large herds of cattle. They sold milk and beef and sometimes rented out their oxen to farmers, who used them to pull their plows. Shepherds tended their calves and talked to their animals with affection.

Far off in the distance were farmyards with hens, geese, ducks, and even pelicans. The farmers fed them well, caring for their flocks in the same way the swamp shepherds looked after their cattle.

Tireless Little Donkeys

While donkeys lived in wild herds in the desert, in the valley of the Nile they helped the peasants carry baskets of wheat and earthenware jars of water. Despite their usefulness, donkeys had a bad reputation. Egyptians linked them to the frightening god Seth. As a precaution, people rarely rode on their donkeys' backs.

Ostrich-Feather Fans

Ostriches lived in the ancient Egyptian desert. They might be the biggest of birds, but they couldn't run fast enough to avoid the arrows of hunters who wanted to kill them for their beautiful feathers. Craftsmen made elegant ostrich-feather fans. Feathers were also the sacred symbol of truth.

CRAFTSMEN AND ARTISTS

KHNUM

There's a legend about the "Day-of-the-First-Time," or the day of creation: "The god Khnum raised the sky and spread the earth on its foundation. The first thing he did after that was to organize all of Egypt. He sat in front of his potter's wheel and shaped and molded with his strong arms and agile fingers. He didn't stop working until he had separated bodies from limbs and had succeeded in forming faces."

When the sun rose, the potter, like the great god, was already at work shaping dozens of jars. All covered with mud, he kneaded the earth, adding bits of finely chopped straw as he went. His potter's wheel whizzed around. In a matter of minutes, the craftsman had fashioned a jar. When he was satisfied with his work, he etched a small mark, or potter's sign, onto the object and let it dry in front of the workshop.

Then he returned to his wheel to begin all over again. At the end of the day, he heated up his oven to bake the day's work.

He made, without a pause, many bowls, platters, jugs, jars, and small cosmetic pots. The pottery might come with or without handles, flat or rounded, wide or narrow, large or small. Styles and shapes varied greatly because Egyptians put their pottery to many different uses. They stored everything in pots: grain, water, beer, oil, and even papyrus.

What Egyptians couldn't store in clay pots, they put in baskets or small lidded

Papyrus paper was a great luxury because it was so difficult to make.

A specialized scribe of the temple might work an entire year to make only half a dozen papyrus scrolls, each one more than 30 feet (10 meters) long.

cases. The basket maker's work began in the marshes where papyrus reeds grew. These plants could grow to be 6 to 8 feet (2 to 2.5 meters) tall. The men cut the stalks and tied them into bales, which they carried home on their backs.

The basket makers sorted the stalks according to size. As a treat while they were working, they nibbled on the tender, sweet shoots of young papyrus. It was the outer rind of the reeds that was woven into baskets, ropes, clothes, bedding, floor mats, and even flimsy combs. It was also used to make cages for ducks and geese. The long, flexible stalks were made into papyrus skiffs. Specialists peeled away the outer rinds and turned the remaining stalks into writing paper.

Making the papyrus scrolls used for writing was a complicated process. The paper maker first cut pieces of papyrus stems lengthwise into very narrow strips. He then flattened these strips with a wooden mallet.

He carefully placed two layers of papyrus strips at right angles on top of a piece of linen. One layer ran horizontally, the other vertically, and the lineup had to be perfect. He moistened the papyrus, covered it with another layer of linen, and then pounded it for a long time. The sap worked like glue to stick the strips together.

When the mixture dried, the scribe had a strong, flexible piece of papyrus paper. After polishing it with a stone, he glued it to other sheets with resin to make a long scroll.

THE CARPENTER'S SHOP

The king's carpenters used cedar, cypress, and juniper from Lebanon and Syria and ebony from the heart of Africa to make expensive furniture, sturdy boats, statues, luxurious coffins, and supporting structures for pyramids. For cheaper furniture, they used local, softer woods.

It was hot in the workshop, and sawdust stuck to the carpenters' sweaty skin. Flies buzzed all around them. Their axes—called adzes—and hammers pounded, and the screeching of their saws reached a deafening pitch. An efficient foreman supervised all the activity in the workshop, and the craftsmen worked wonders. They knew how to decorate caskets or chests with bright paintings, inlaid ivory, and stone or glass.

Many poor Egyptians didn't enjoy these luxurious objects. Their belongings were limited to a bed, baskets, mats, pottery, and perhaps a three-legged stool or a small chest made of sycamore.

Although sycamore trees were plentiful in Egypt, their wood was of low quality. The same was true of palm trees, whose trunks were used to make beams and whose leaves were turned into baskets, mats, and brooms.

SCULPTORS

The craftsmen of Egypt showed amazing skill at working materials with copper and, later, bronze tools. Nowhere, however, did they shine more than in the cutting and carving of stone.

The entire Nile Valley served as a vast quarry for the limestone and granite used to raise walls. Fine stones used for vessels and statues and semiprecious stones for jewelry came from the Eastern Desert.

Extracting the stone, whether it was buried deep within a mountain cave or was in a wide-open quarry, was always a tough job. Tools were very basic and made of wood, flint, stones, copper, or bronze.

Once the stone block was taken from the quarry and measured, the sculptors went to work. They carved the stone into a shape with copper chisels and wooden hammers. This took much time and physical strength. They then polished the statue with sand and abrasive powder. Finally, with pointed tools, they carved the details of the hair, eyes, clothing, and ornaments.

The size of their work varied from that of a tiny figurine to that of a figure of such monumental proportions that even the passage of thousands of years has not dulled the effect. These sculptures represented the many gods and goddesses who peopled the Egyptian world, as well as rulers and nobility, ordinary men and women, family scenes, and even animals.

Through these masterpieces in stone the ancient Egyptians come alive for us today. They provide clues about how these people lived and what they loved, feared, and hoped for.

PAINTERS

Many Egyptian homes had paintings on their walls and even on their ceilings. The inside of the temples radiated with gold-covered obelisks (pillars) and bright paintings that covered the walls and columns. Royal tombs had rich, dark blue ceilings dotted with glistening gold stars. Deeper in the tomb, between the inner walls, were statues of kings, queens, servants, and deities.

When the sculptors had finished their task, the scribes and painters went to work. They brightened up the carvings, statues, and scenes on the walls. Men had brown skin; women

had yellow complexions. The brightly colored, cheerful paintings made it seem that the ancient Egyptians lived a very good life. This may have been the truth about their lives, or, perhaps, this was how they dreamed life could be.

JEWELERS

Far away from mines and construction sites, other artists created marvelous objects. With very simple tools they worked blue turquoise, white ivory, green malachite, and dark blue lapis lazuli.

In well-guarded workshops, goldsmiths cut precious stones and melted gold to make beautiful jewelry. Rich Egyptians, men and women alike, wore diadems, or headbands, earrings, necklaces, bracelets, and rings. The king himself loved jewelry. There is even an ancient Egyptian saying that goes: The skin of kings is made of gold, their bones of silver, and their hair of lapis lazuli.

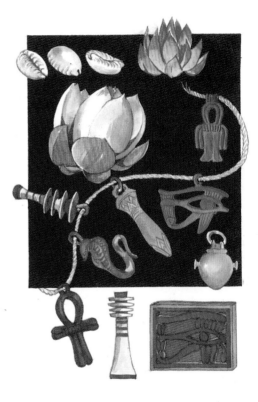

What Is an Amulet?

Amulets are pieces of jewelry that are shaped to resemble gods, goddesses, royal emblems, or some protective symbol. Ancient Egyptians thought that the more amulets they were buried with, the more they were magically protected from the many thousands of dangers in this world and in the afterlife.

SCRIBES AND SCHOLARS

For most of Egyptian history, more than seven hundred different characters were used to write on papyrus scrolls, temple walls, statues, and vases. These astonishing strings of little drawings have revealed many aspects of Egyptian life to us.

This writing, called hieroglyphic, was beautiful by necessity. For the ancient Egyptians, the writing of some words re-created the objects they described. These were called pictographs. The more beautiful the writing, the more real and powerful the object became. Signs representing dangerous animals were sometimes cut in half to make the animals harmless. Many other signs were used to represent sounds. Some of these were alphabetic signs, which stood for one letter. Other signs stood for two or three letters.

Scribes were much more than simply people who knew how to write. The complexity and beauty of their language demanded that they be scholars and artists.

However, such beauty, which was essential to important historical and religious texts, was not needed for everyday writing. When it came to ordinary documents, such as letters, livestock registers, and ledgers, scribes wrote very fast. Instead of writing on expensive papyrus paper, they used limestone fragments or pieces of broken pottery.

When hieroglyphs were written so quickly, they looked altogether different. Hieratic, as this simplified running script was called, was the same language, but the little drawings were converted into dashes, strokes, and curves. It was written with ink and the tips of reeds.

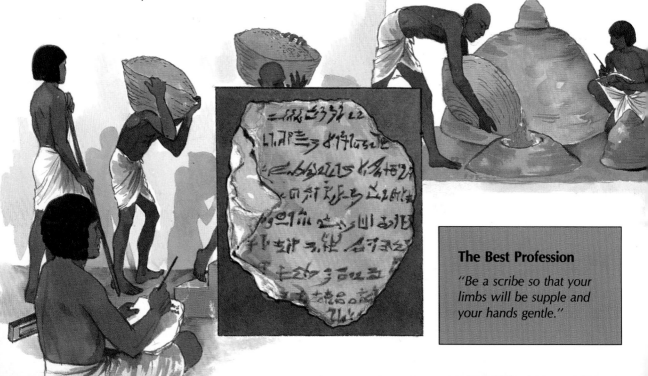

The Best Profession

"Be a scribe so that your limbs will be supple and your hands gentle."

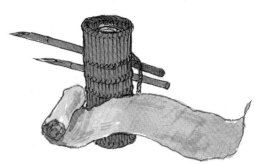

Scribes had lots of work because they were responsible for the smooth operation of the whole kingdom. Everything depended on them. They drafted reports and detailed accounts, transmitted and supervised the execution of the king's orders, calculated and collected taxes, drew up legal documents, and wrote letters for other people.

They worked in the temples to re-copy religious texts that influenced how the country was run. They wanted to be sure that the words of the gods were preserved. The scribes also wrote instructions to guide the dead in the afterlife.

Scribes were responsible for the writing on amulets. They wrote down magic spells that would protect the living from sickness and harassment by the ill-meaning spirits of the dead.

Scribes also wrote stories, poems, and fables that both taught and entertained the people. And they amused themselves by writing long, humorous works that made fun of all the professions, including their own.

Medou Netcher

Egyptians called their writing Medou netcher, which means "the words of the god," or "divine words." The word hiero-glyph was used much later by the Greeks. It means "sacred writing."

Thoth the Scholar

Thoth, god of the moon, was an intellectual with an ibis bird's head. He was the patron of scribes and the inventor of hieroglyphs.

TRAINING TO BE A SCRIBE

Writings have been discovered between parents and their children and teachers and their students that tell us about the seriousness of a scribe's education. Here is a father's advice to his son:

"I sent you to school with the children of high-ranking civil servants to master the skills that would bring you power and authority. Write with your hands, speak with your mouth, and accept advice. Don't give up. Do what your teacher tells you. Obey."

At the age of nine, some children were singled out from the rest of the children, who continued in their undisciplined play in the fields. They were sent to a special school for scribes where they spent years learning to read, write, and do math. But it was mostly boys who learned these skills, and girls often remained illiterate.

Schoolmasters were strict and often used sticks on their pupils. "As I see it," wrote a scribe teacher to a student, "you are nothing but a stupid fool. I will make a man out of you, you little scoundrel."

The students sat cross-legged on the classroom floor and listened to their teacher. Many of them resisted their strict schooling at first and received lashings and scoldings for their rebellious behavior. But their teachers and parents told them over and over that they were better off than the children who would grow up to labor in the fields and workshops. So they usually settled down to learn the lessons that prepared them to become a scribe.

In the morning, the scribe teacher listened to the students as together they recited long texts. Every day he assigned them compositions, math problems, and complex writing exercises. Pupils wrote on rough pieces of broken pottery, on fragments of limestone, and on slabs of sycamore coated with a thin layer of plaster. They drew hieroglyphs with

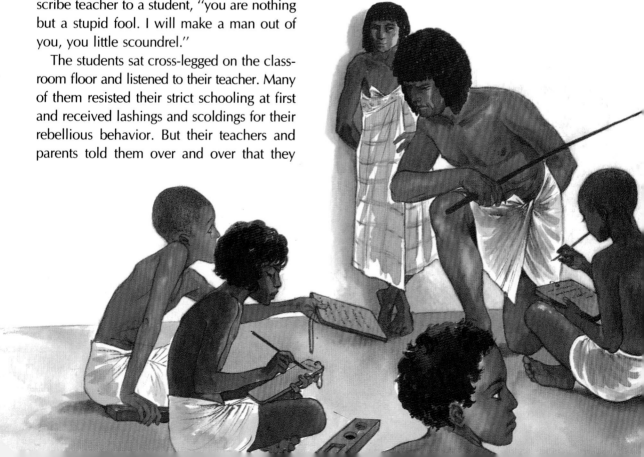

reed tips dipped into pots of red and black ink. Their writing tablets were washed so often that they were always in need of a new coat of plaster.

The teacher paid close attention to the rustling of the reed pens. In the beginning, students made lots of mistakes, such as misspelling words, leaving them out altogether, and shaping the hieroglyphs badly. It was a difficult job because they had to be able to write from left to right, from right to left, and from top to bottom.

This strict, formal training lasted roughly four years. Finally, the big day came when they were entrusted with writing on papyrus. Then it was time to complete their education by doing an apprenticeship, which meant training for several more years under a master scribe.

Two Kinds of Hieroglyphs

The Egyptian system of writing was hieroglyphic. This means that they used pictures to express ideas. These hieroglyphs, or pictures, were divided into two different kinds of signs. Ideograms provided information about the words they represented. Phonograms were expressions of sounds. For example, a drawing of a mouth stood for the sound "r."

A Profitable Profession

Those royal scribes who worked in the pharaoh's palace lived in conditions of unimaginable luxury. Even those who lived far from the capital made a very good living. On the whole, scribes were better off than other people.

A SCHOLARLY PROFESSION

"Put your heart into your books and love them as you do your mother because there is nothing in this world of greater value than books," advised an old scribe who was proud of his profession and proud of the knowledge he possessed.

Scribes worked long hours because they had many difficult questions to ponder. How to build a temple with giant columns? How to dig a well? How to weigh and measure? How to haul heavy objects? They were always thinking, looking for solutions to problems, and trying to make progress.

The first scribes developed a system for working with numbers that was simple but rather awkward. Addition and subtraction were easy enough. But they only knew how to multiply by two, or to add numbers by doubling them. They hadn't yet discovered division, so they divided numbers through a series of subtractions. Nor did zero exist.

Imagine a scribe seated in front of his white limestone board, trying to solve a complex math problem. He would have to carry out a series of multiplications by two. Even after he found the solution, the hardest part was yet to come—the division. He would begin by doing a series of multiplications by two, trying different smaller numbers that might multiply into the larger number he already knew.

The night sky, too, was an object of study for the scribes. They drew maps locating and naming the constellations of stars. They called the Big Dipper the Ox Leg, and they even named the planet Mars Red Horus.

This knowledge of the sky, like all sciences, was very useful to the Egyptians. For instance, it helped them decide which way a new temple or pyramid should face. It was also useful in drawing up the list of lucky

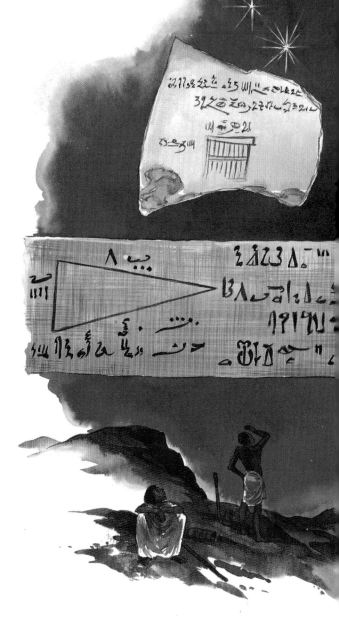

An Old Calendar

The Egyptian calendar was used by the Greeks centuries later. Next the Romans copied the Greek calendar. Scholars of the Middle Ages then copied it from the Romans, and so, in turn, did we!

Geometry Wizards

The pharaoh employed scribe-mathematicians who knew how to figure out the surface area of rectangular, square, and even circular fields. They knew how to measure the surface area of a circle based on the length of its diameter. In this way, the king knew exactly the amount of taxes owed him.

and unlucky days, their version of our horoscope, and it became the basis for designing their calendar.

Egyptian scribes made such accurate observations and calculations that they invented a 365-day calendar. They divided it into twelve months of thirty days each and tacked on five extra days at the end of the year.

Signs and Numbers

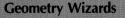

For example, 1,432 was written:

Zero didn't exist, but the scribes left an empty space for it. So, 303 was written:

PHARAOH RULES THE LAND

The pharaoh owned all of Egypt: its fields, deserts, canals, mines, people, animals, and even the Nile River. His life was dedicated to watching over and protecting his kingdom. Needless to say, this was an enormous job.

One single man, the king, was responsible for laying down the law, filling the treasury, honoring the deities, winning wars, and maintaining order. The pharaoh chose one or two viziers, or prime ministers, to help him. But he was often suspicious of their ambition.

It was usually the pharaoh's son who succeeded, or followed, him to the throne. He was trained to excel in sports and to be an expert in the field of battle from the time he was very young. Sometimes the son would even serve along with his aging father to gain experience before the pharaoh died.

But the transfer of power was not always smooth. Rivalries and secret plots could change the orderly passage from one pharaoh to the next. Egyptian history is a com-plex story of thirty royal dynasties ruling for more than three thousand years, and some troubled periods of chaos when royal power was divided or weakened.

Strength was the key to keeping the royal dynasty in power. In large part, the king's power came from the people's belief that he was a god. The king also backed up this divine right to rule by controlling the country with his armed forces. In its most basic form, this strength was shown through the physical power of the king. As one scribe

wrote, "Pharaoh was so strong that nobody, not a single one of his soldiers, nor any of the foreign leaders, could draw his bow."

There were no laws that forbade women from ruling. However, there were only four female pharaohs in the three thousand years of Egyptian history.

Hatshepsut, the most famous of these women, reigned for twenty years beginning in 1500 B.C. As the daughter, sister, and wife of kings, she knew well how to be a strong ruler. She built beautiful monuments and sent her army on long expeditions in search of rare goods from far-off lands.

There was no doubt, though, that Egyptians preferred a man to rule their kingdom. The pharaoh's most important role was to serve as a lawmaker and warrior. Women rulers knew this. Hatshepsut's artists sometimes painted her with a man's body and a woman's head, and she would appear before her subjects wearing an ornamental fake beard. She led her troops into battle with Nubia, the land south of Egypt.

The Royal Crown

At the beginning of their history, when the two kingdoms of Upper and Lower Egypt became united, a double crown representing both kingdoms was designed.

Fear of the Pharaoh

"I came before his Majesty on his throne of gold," an Egyptian man wrote. "I kissed the ground below his feet. Stretched out on the ground, I began to feel weak. I lost control of my limbs, my heart lept in my chest, and, then—I fainted."

THE PHARAOH'S SOLDIERS

Personal strength was important, but without the backing of an army, a pharaoh would never have been able to police his borders, collect his taxes, and control the people of Egypt.

The army ensured that order was maintained throughout the kingdom, and, according to one scribe, it "spread fear of the pharaoh into foreign lands." Above all, the scribe continues, Egyptian soldiers had to be "so well disciplined that not one of them strikes a comrade, snatches bread from a passer-by, or steals clothing in a village."

In the New Kingdom, or Empire Period, which lasted from 1570 to 1085 B.C., the army's top group was the chariotry—the wealthy knights who drove the king's chariots. Two strong horses pulled the vehicles that held two men: the charioteer, who drove the horses, and the warrior, who fought with a bow and arrow and a spear. It was a dangerous job. Soldiers often fell off the chariots and suffered serious wounds.

Infantrymen, or foot soldiers, made up a large part of the army. The same scribe tells us how Egyptians were hardened to the life of a soldier: "They were taken away as children and kept in camps. They were kicked in the stomach, knocked over by blows to the face, and punched in the eye."

"Let me tell you about a march to Syria," continues the mocking scribe, "to a country in the desert, each soldier carrying his food and water on his shoulders. . . . By the time the soldiers arrived in front of the enemy, they were like trapped birds, without a drop of energy left in their bodies."

The soldier's fate hardly seemed desirable. However, if he demonstrated great courage in battle, he was decorated with a gold badge of courage. He might also be given part of the booty, captured men or women to work

for him, or even the income from a good plot of land. And then, between military campaigns, soldiers led comfortable, protected lives.

Furthermore, war was only one part of military life. Soldiers waged war for the king, but they also organized expeditions to faraway lands. When the pharaoh wanted gold, ebony, or ivory, the army went off on long merchant voyages to find it for him. When the pharaoh wanted a new temple built or obelisks erected, it was the army who organized the workmen in the quarries and oversaw the transportation of the heavy stone blocks. When the pharaoh needed protec-

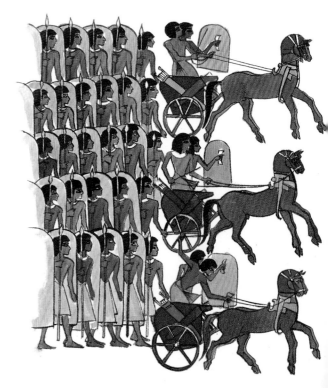

tion, his best soldiers guarded his palace, and those who were experienced in the desert were sent to patrol the borders of the kingdom.

Soldiers served as policemen, customs officers, miners, and construction foremen. They were devoted to their king and would do anything to increase his glory.

Horses at Last!

Egyptians didn't begin using horses until about 1600 B.C., when they were introduced from western Asia.

Counting the Dead

To count how many of their soldiers had died on the battlefield, one hand was cut off of each dead body. A scribe counted the pile of hands. There were as many dead soldiers as there were hands.

SLAVES AND PRISONERS

Slavery became an accepted institution in ancient Egypt as a result of many successful foreign wars in which the defeated people were brought back to Egypt as slaves. The following story shows how common it was to buy and sell slaves.

"In 1275 B.C., the 15th year of Ramses II's reign, Reia the merchant came to me with a Syrian slave named Gem-ny-her-Imentet, who was still a young girl. He said, 'Buy this girl from me at a fair price.' I took the girl and gave Reia a fine linen blanket, a sheet, a coat, three loin cloths, a skirt, five bronze containers, a bit of copper, a pot of honey, and ten tunics."

The girl was probably born of a slave captured during a military campaign against Syria. During such campaigns, the king brought back many prisoners of war, as well as precious objects and military arms. He gave some of the prisoners to his best generals. Others were placed in the service of a temple, at construction sites, or in the mines and quarries.

In the mines, the captured slaves mixed with Egyptian prisoners, who were thieves, criminals, or runaways. In Egypt, the entire family might be held hostage along with the criminal.

Slaves could be sold, inherited, loaned, or rented. They could also be emancipated, or freed, at which time they were as free as any of the pharaoh's subjects. Male slaves could marry free women, accumulate personal belongings, and even hire servants. When a male slave died, his children inherited his possessions.

The Bible tells the story of Joseph, the Israelite whose brothers sold him into slavery. In Egypt, Joseph was bought by a rich man named Potiphar. Little by little, Joseph became Potiphar's trusted confidant.

One day, after being slandered by his master's wife, Joseph was put in prison. The Bible tells us that his God, Lord of the Jews, decided to help him. The chief prison guard trusted Joseph and gave him some important responsibilities. Joseph was even asked to interpret the dreams of noble Egyptians imprisoned in the same jail.

Upon learning of this, the pharaoh summoned Joseph. His interpretations of the king's dreams and his advice on important matters demonstrated his intelligence, wisdom, and goodness. The pharaoh gave him a ring, a gold necklace, fine linen clothing, a chariot, an Egyptian name, and a wife. In several years' time, Joseph, the poor Jewish slave, had become the king's adviser.

The Pharaoh's Good Intentions

In 720 B.C., poverty had become so widespread in Egypt that the king took pity on his subjects. The pharaoh Bocchoris decided to do away with the old traditional punishment that made slaves of those unable to pay their debts.

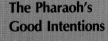

HOW THE PHARAOH LIVED

The pharaoh was in a unique position. He had sole responsibility for the workings of the universe as it was known to the Egyptians. He was both a king and a god to them. Everything was under his care, for it all belonged to him. A scribe wrote of his pharaoh, "His eyes scrutinize [look carefully at] the depths of his subjects. All that he orders is done."

"Ruling is a good profession," stated the king Khety. And truly, the king lived in tremendous luxury, surrounded by hundreds of

servants and beautiful women. If his military responsibilities weighed too heavily on him, he could assign his power to a general. If he didn't like his administrative duties, a vizier would act in his name. Priests presided in his name if he asked. The pharaoh could give as much of his work as he wished to others.

On a typical day, following the morning's rituals, the king listened to a scribe read the daily dispatches. He would ponder any decisions that needed to be made, ask for advice if he needed it, and then dictate his responses to his scribes.

Often, the pharaoh traveled, for both business and pleasure. He owned many royal homes in different locations. When he sailed on the Nile, he rode on a luxurious royal bark, and all the members of his family and court traveled with him. The king, of course, was set apart from his passengers in a special cabin. Thin, see-through curtains kept flies and mosquitoes out, while inviting gentle breezes to pass through.

He might be traveling to inspect a construction site. The pharaoh watched the building of his tomb or a new temple very closely. Or, he might be on his way to hunt in the desert or in the marshlands on the banks of the Nile.

Yet he always returned to the seat of power, his palace in the capital city of Memphis. During both the Old and New Kingdoms,

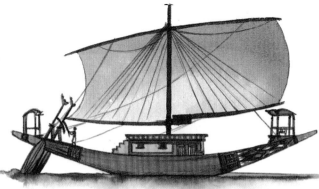

when scribes wrote the word "city," they were referring to Memphis, the political center of Egypt and the chief residence of the king.

THE PHARAOH'S WIVES

The queen was thought of as a goddess, but her title of Great Royal Wife illustrated her relation to her husband. The children of the pharaoh and his queen were, in principle, the only heirs to the throne. The queen was the highest-ranking dignitary in the kingdom besides her husband. She often ruled for her son when the pharaoh died, until the prince was old enough to marry and govern the land.

Dressed Like a King!

According to writings and drawings, the pharaoh dazzled all who saw him. He carried two scepters, sported a fake beard, and wore a double crown decorated with the cobra and vulture goddesses, which were supposed to protect him. And yet, the mummy of the famous King Ramses II shows him to have been in truth a very short, small-boned man.

The pharaoh, however, did not have just one wife. He also had several less important wives who, together, made up his royal harem. He would often marry for political reasons. For instance, he might take a foreign princess as one of his wives to firm up an agreement with a neighboring country.

His wives spent their time making themselves beautiful, singing in temples, dancing, raising their children, and, sometimes, thinking up secret plots so that one of their children, rather than one of the Great Royal Wife's, would inherit the throne.

TIME TO RELAX

At sunset when the heat became bearable, the pharaoh and his friends would retreat to a large dining hall to eat, tell stories, and have a good time. The servants had been preparing the feast for hours in the kitchen. Pretty servants carried in the different courses: grilled meats and fish, crisp vegetables, cakes, fruits, and sweets. Wine and beer flowed freely, and laughter grew louder as the evening wore on.

Men and women sat on stools and chairs scattered around the room. Everybody ate with their fingers. A servant stood by, ready to bring a jug of water and a dish when they were ready to wash the food from their hands. Another servant held a large basin, ready to rush toward a guest who was sick from too much rich food and drink. This was accepted

behavior among Egyptians. It was also customary for them to wear flowers and scented cones of fat on their heads, which melted and ran down their faces as the room heated up.

Lovely dancers, dressed in gauzy, flowing robes, enchanted the spectators. Some musicians played oboes and flutes; others sang and beat on tambourines or shook oval rattles called sistrums; or they might pluck gently on the strings of lutes or harps.

In the daytime, Egyptians relaxed by playing board games. They were especially fond of a game called Snake. They sat around a stone board shaped like a curled snake whose

Cones of Fat

Small scented cones of fat attached to wigs gave off a sweet perfume. In the heat of the room, the fat melted and slid down the face and body, which softened the skin.

head lay in the center. Its long body was divided into squares, half of which were hollowed out. Six pieces shaped like lions and lionesses and many marbles were needed to play. Unfortunately, they didn't write down instructions on how to play this interesting game.

Egyptians liked another board game similar to checkers, which they called Senet, and a game they called Hound and Jackal. They also loved to ask one another riddles and to play a sort of hot-or-cold game, in which one player hid a stone or stick under one of several pots and the others had to guess where it was.

The Sad Music of the Harpist

Nobles were especially pleased to find a harpist, blinded by an eye infection, to pluck the strings of his instrument at their parties. This was how the nobles made sure that they alone could admire the princesses and beautiful dancers.

A MAGICAL LAND

Ancient Egyptians were threatened by strange and menacing forces. People suffered when the Nile flooded too much or too little or an unexpected drought destroyed the year's crop. When sickness, famine, and death came upon the Egyptians, they were afraid. They believed that only unearthly beings could have the power to help them. And so the Egyptians tried to please these beings—their gods.

The pharaoh's kingdom was protected by dozens of deities. It was truly a land of magic. Speech was the simplest form of this magic. Egyptians believed that to pronounce a word was to create an object. For them, the creation of the world and the word were intertwined.

As the legend goes, the great god Ptah spoke in the very first days of the world's existence. Creatures and things came into being at their very mention. In the same way, drawing or sculpting animals was thought to bring them to life.

Such beliefs presented real practical advantages. Fake stone doors in tombs allowed the deceased to come and go as

they pleased. A table full of food painted on a wall was enough to ensure that the dead had plenty to eat.

Sometimes though, when people's lives were threatened, words were needed as a power to ward off evil spirits. For instance, when Egyptians fell ill, they believed that their sickness had been directed by evil spirits or brought on by their own bad deeds. They sought to protect themselves by saying magic spells or prayers to their favorite gods and goddesses.

Scribe-doctors relied on both medical skills and magical remedies to cure their patients. They knew a great deal about the organs and their functions, but it was just as important to say a magical spell or to write on an amulet or charm, which the doctor hung on a seven-knotted necklace around his patient's neck.

Foresighted Egyptians didn't always wait until they were ill to seek medical protection. They traveled to small chapels in the desert, where dangerous snakes and scorpions tended to collect. Inside were statues that priests had covered with magic spells to protect those who entered from the deadly venoms. People poured cool running water over the heads of the statues to absorb the power of the magic spells. They then drank

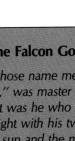

Horus the Falcon God

Horus, whose name means "faraway," was master of the sky. It was he who created light with his two eyes, the sun and the moon. His father was the sky god Osiris, and his mother was Isis, Mistress of Magic.

Magic for All

Everyone—princes and peasants alike—used magic spells. Even the king relied on magic to protect his family, his subjects, and all his kingdom.

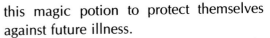

this magic potion to protect themselves against future illness.

Sometimes, when a patient was very sick, the scribe-doctor's only recourse was that of a direct cry for help to a great god. One such doctor wrote down his spell: "Out poison, come spread yourself on the ground! Horus casts you out, destroys you, spits on you. You fall, you are weak, you are defeated."

The scribe-doctor might grow more insistent and even threaten the deity with terrible revenge if he didn't heal the sick person: "Nobody will bring you offerings in the temple! You will receive no more white bread and no more meat!"

In the Hands of the Gods

"All that happens is in the hands of the gods" was a saying that scribes commonly etched into beautiful jewelry. And in the land of the pharaoh, there was no shortage of gods. There were hundreds of great gods and goddesses, lesser known local gods, and familiar spirits.

A particular god's character would vary from one region to the next. The form of a god was also subject to change. This was true of the sun god Re (pronounced "ray"), who was known as Khepri the scarab beetle at sunrise, Re-Harakhty the great hawk at noon, and Atum the ram-headed man at sunset.

It can be difficult to trace the identity of the gods through their many forms and local personalities. And then, over the three thousand years of Egyptian civilization, their stories evolved, so much so that the history of the Egyptian gods wanders like a maze back through time.

Animal Gods

Temples were built to house the gods, who were represented by statues and totem animals with semi-human characteristics. Artists were very skilled in forming this strange mixture of anatomy. They were able to mix the body of a man or a woman with the head of an animal so that the statue appeared both graceful and natural.

These animals might be beneficial ones, such as Hathor the cow god and Khnum the ram god, or they could be dangerous, as were Sobek the crocodile god and Apophis the snake god. In spite of the Egyptians' belief in animal-like gods, they didn't consider all of these animals to be sacred. There were no laws against killing crocodiles or eating beef.

However, in late Egyptian history, the cult of sacred animals became part of the ritual in the temple. Certain animals were raised to live protected within its walls and given special religious burials when they died.

The Human Side of the Gods

In the countryside and villages far away from the great gods and splendid temples, Egyptians felt closer to minor deities. There, people asked for help of the gods they felt close to. Here is one Egyptian's prayer: "The minor deity Mertseger [a goddess of a local mountain peak] lends a hand to those who love her and to those who hold her in their heart."

One way to understand these ancient people is to study the names they gave to their children. Through the magic of a first name, Egyptians thanked great gods, protected against future dangers, or simply used their imaginations. Boys might be called Ptahmose, which means "son of Ptah," the patron of

craftsmen, or Neferenpet, which means "good year." Girls were often given poetic names, such as Tamit, "the cat"; Oubekhet, "the bright one"; or Nefertiti, "the pretty one has arrived."

Egyptian children were named after gods; and, in spite of their great powers, gods could behave in very human ways. Although they had many good qualities, they could also have human weaknesses. There are many stories about their lies, fights, trickery, plots, and assassinations.

Legends describe the gods with humor and realism. Jealousy between the brothers Osiris and Seth led to the murder of Osiris. Thirst for power drove Isis to lie to the great sun god Re. Hathor, goddess of love and protector of the dead, was usually pictured as a nurturing cow. But one time she turned into a roaring lioness and drank so much beer that she got drunk! Clearly, the life of the gods was very much like that of men and women.

SETH

OSIRIS

TEMPLES, HOMES FOR THE GODS

In prehistoric times, reed huts with rounded roofs served as dwellings for the gods. As time went by, Egyptians began to design more elaborate temples. They replaced reeds with mud bricks, and later they began to build with stone.

During the New Kingdom, around 1500 B.C., temples became grand and lavishly decorated. They rose up near the Nile and were often connected to it by a wide avenue leading to a special walkway along the river. Sphinxes—lions with the head of a man, a ram, or a hawk—crouched on their haunches in a long line on either side of the avenue and protected a heavy door in the middle of the temple's pylon, the two towering sides of the gateway. Flags on top of tall poles fluttered in the wind in front of the pylon. Stately obelisks, gradually tapering pillars, reached for the sky, and huge statues of pharaohs also stood at the temple's gates. These enormous structures were decorated with bright colors and were sometimes covered with thin plates of gold engraved with scenes or stories.

The temple's entrance led to a series of courtyards whose ceilings were held up by

many large columns. Some of them had dark blue ceilings embedded with shining golden stars. Nearby, a sacred lake, a well, study rooms, workshops, and gardens ensured that the god and his priests led a pleasant life.

The god's personal belongings, such as small boats, banners, clothing, and dishes, were all kept in small inner rooms. At the very center of the temple, in a small closed sanctuary, was the divine statue. This room, called the holy of holies, was closed to all but the priests and the kings.

"Great God, Wake in Peace."

Priests approached the temple at dawn. They burned incense, opened the doors to the temple's sanctuary, and recited, "The binding seal on this door has been broken. All my wickedness has been put aside. I am pure." They greeted the statue by bowing before it. "Wake in peace," they sang, "great god, wake in peace. May this morning's awakening be peaceful."

The priests performed the god's daily purification and decorated the statue. Then they brought him a breakfast of bread, meat, wine, and water. When they left the sanctuary, someone trailed behind them sweeping the floor. They wanted to erase any trace of their human presence in the sacred room. The midday and evening rituals also took up much of the priests' time.

On holidays, the procession of the divine statue was the most important part of the ceremonies. Egyptians who had never set foot in the temple could see for themselves "the divine beauty of its master, its god."

When the priests carried the statue, decorated with amulets and gold necklaces, to the sanctuary's entrance, the awed crowd fell silent. Sometimes the priests placed the statue aboard a real river vessel for a long procession on the Nile or in the god's sacred lake. Each year the statue of the goddess Hathor spent two weeks in Horus's temple, more than one hundred miles from her home.

Peasants and craftsmen took advantage of these processions to pray to the god and ask for his advice. If the priests carrying the statue stepped forward, the answer to their question was yes, but if they stepped back, it was no.

The priests played a key role in Egyptian life because they were responsible for keeping the gods happy. If they succeeded, the gods allowed life to go on as it had for centuries. If they didn't please the gods, the kingdom was bound to return to the time of the Waters of Chaos that had existed before the creation of the world.

However, the priests always served in the name of the pharaoh. In theory, only the king could act as an intermediary between men and gods. The pharaoh claimed to be the son of god, which made him part god himself. So, although the priests helped the pharaoh, who could not in practice serve as the high priest in all the temples of Egypt, it was the pharaoh who bore the real responsibility for his kingdom.

Sphinxes

Sphinxes were symbols of divine power. They had a huge lion's body and either the head of a ram or hawk or that of the king or queen whose palace or temple they protected.

Purification of the Gods

Every morning, priests sprinkled fresh water on the divine statue. Then they coated it with perfumed oils, clothed it, painted its face, and adorned it with jewels and amulets.

Prophets

The most powerful priests were called First Prophets of the God. It was their job to oversee the temple and surrounding lands in the name of the king who had appointed them. The chief priests were assisted by many specialized priests who copied the religious documents, studied the stars, carried the divine boat, prepared offerings, and kept the books. All these people dedicated their lives to the gods and their kingdom.

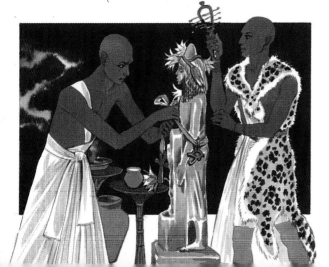

PYRAMIDS TO HOUSE THE DEAD

Egyptians strongly believed in an afterlife and did everything they could to prepare both the burial place and the body of the dead person so that the spirits of the dead would be happy.

During the Old Kingdom, it was only the kings and queens who built pyramids to serve as burial places. These enormous structures were perhaps designed to look like the piles of sand and rock that once marked prehistoric tombs.

Early tombs were nothing more than simple holes dug in the earth. Underneath the pyramid, corridors and shafts led to the tomb containing the royal coffin and to rooms filled with supplies and furniture. While the tomb was being built, workers brought in lamps and torches so that they could work in the dark. After the burial, the workers sealed off the corridors and filled in the entrance. The surrounding wall protected the pyramid as well as the nearby mortuary temple where funeral services were held. Religious spells were carved on the walls of the tomb so that the dead person's voyage into the afterlife would go smoothly.

Although we suspect that the shape and size of Egyptian monuments had religious

significance, we will never know for sure why the ancients built these huge structures as they did. Possibly, the pyramid was an image of the mound that rose from the ocean on the Day-of-the-First-Time, when the universe came into being. The earliest pyramids may also have represented gigantic stairways that the dead kings climbed to reach the gods. The edges where the four triangular sides come together seem like the rays of the sun shining down on the earth, offering the dead person a path to heaven.

Old Kingdom nobility had flat-topped rectangular stone tombs called "mastabas" built around the royal pyramid. As time went on, though, and the pharaoh's power decreased, these mastabas became fancier and they were scattered far away from the royal burial spots.

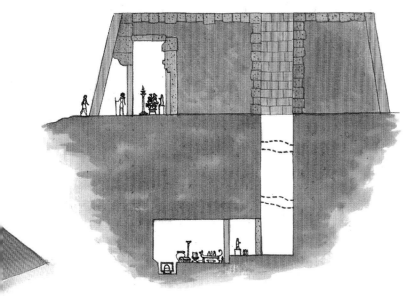

Pyramid Builders

Because tombs were located at the bottom of deep, vertical shafts, the builders of both mastabas and pyramids developed sophisticated techniques for digging into the stone floor of the desert with tools made of stone, wood, and copper. But pyramids were expensive and took a long time to build. In the most recent of the Egyptian kingdoms, kings and noblemen had their tombs tunneled into the sides of barren cliffs. They took advantage of mountains that formed natural pyramids reaching for the sky.

Digging these mountainside tombs was still a difficult task, but it was easier and quicker than building a pyramid from the ground up. Workers built stairways on the mountain slope leading up to the face of the cliff, which served as the outer wall. If there was enough room, they built a small interior courtyard studded with columns. They dug out one or two rooms that opened into a narrow vertical shaft leading down into the tomb. The rock walls and ceiling of the burial chamber were perfect for painting scenes

Big and Little Pyramids

Although the pharaohs of the Old Kingdom had enormous pyramids built, in later times, when the kings had less power and wealth, only common Egyptians built their own pyramids. These were very small and sat on top of their mortuary, or funeral, chapels.

about the passage of the dead king into the company of the gods. The inside walls of the chapels were decorated with beautiful paintings of scenes from daily life or the hoped-for meeting with gods in the afterlife.

Buried Treasure

On the day the pharaoh's body was buried, the shaft leading to the tomb was closed off. The king's coffin lay inside the tomb surrounded by the offerings of jewels, weapons, clothing, furniture, and any other items that might make his life after death enjoyable. Gold, silver, bronze, precious stones, and delicate fabrics were among the precious objects selected. The richer the dead person, the greater the treasure. Amulets, precious objects, scrolls, writings, and drawings protected the dead with their magic powers. Sometimes even a map of the underworld was included. In later years, the spells and maps were preserved on beautifully decorated papyrus scrolls. These have become known as The Books of the Dead.

Everyone knew that these riches lay within the temple tombs. And some very poor Egyptians must have dreamed about these unguarded, buried treasures.

Some desperate people dared to ignore the magical power of the amulets and images of gods protecting the dead. They broke in to rob the royal tombs. Some dug out sand and rocks and tried to get in through the shaft. Others burrowed straight through the mountainside to reach the tomb by a more direct route.

This kind of illegal activity was dangerous for many reasons. However, the temptation was so strong that robbers risked accidents,

wild animals roaming the desert at night, the wrath of desert gods, and the sudden appearance of the police.

These robberies probably multiplied as the extravagance of the pyramids increased. We think that many royal tombs were also robbed in much later times. Almost the only tombs left untouched were those of priests, scribes, and servants. Through studying these, we have been able to uncover many valuable clues about this highly developed, fascinating civilization.

Four Sons of Horus

MUMMIES

Egyptians believed that if bodies were pre-served, the dead would continue to exist in the afterlife. Mummification was a long and involved process, and several different meth-ods were used. These ranged from simpler procedures that the middle class could afford to costly ones available only to the rich.

To mummify a wealthy or royal body, embalmers began by removing the brain, lungs, stomach, liver, heart, and intestines. They threw out the brain but placed the heart, wrapped up, back into the chest cav-ity. They put the rest of the organs in pretty alabaster jars called canopic jars, with stop-pers sculpted to represent the four sons of Horus. They then carefully washed the body, filled it with scented resins, and placed it in a tub of crystals to dry it out. This bath lasted for seventy days.

Next, the embalmers wrapped the body with long linen bandages. They were careful

The Four Sons of Horus

As the legend goes, "The four sons of the god Horus performed the funeral rites for their grandfather Osiris. They cried and opened his mouth with their bronze fingers so that he could eat and speak." Horus's sons, who have the heads of a monkey, a man, a jackal, and a falcon, adorned the lids of the canopic jars that preserved the organs of the dead.

to place magical amulets in key spots to help the dead person along the path to eternity. Then, another layer of bandages was dipped in perfumed liquid resin and wrapped around the body. Once all these steps were completed, embalmers placed the mummy in its coffin and the burial rites began.

LIFE AFTER DEATH

Egyptian burial ceremonies were very carefully planned. Mourners hovered over the pharaoh's mummy. They moaned and cried. The more mourners there were at a funeral, the greater the status of the dead became. For this reason, people took to hiring women who would wail and thrash about in a dramatic display of sorrow.

A long funeral procession moved slowly, with the royal family at its head, toward the tomb. Priests read from religious works. Incense burners gave off a pleasant fragrance, and sistrums resonated sadly. Those who carried the offerings struggled along on the hot desert sands.

Finally, the procession arrived at the entrance to the tomb. The queen would pronounce her farewell to the dead person, and the last, most important, ritual was performed. This was called the "opening of the

mouth." A ritual adz was placed on the mummy's nose, eyes, ears, and mouth to revive the dead person's spirit. This ritual satisfied the mourners that they had prepared the way for the dead person to be transformed into a god. The workers then closed the tomb forever.

One of the oldest beliefs of the Egyptians was that Osiris, after being assassinated, chose to live in the afterlife. As god of the dead, he presided over the court of those who had recently died.

According to legend, Osiris used a scale to weigh the amount of good and bad in each person. On one side of the scale was the dead person's heart, and on the other side was the feather of truth, the goddess Maat. If the heart balanced equally with truth, the scale would tip in the right direction and the dead person would be allowed to enjoy the afterlife. If the scale tipped the other way, though, the Devourer would eat him up.

Those who survived the journey to the afterlife were given a field in the land of Osiris. They spent the rest of eternity planting seeds, irrigating, and harvesting crops. But in

Maat

Maat, daughter of the great sun god Re, was goddess of justice and truth. This pretty young woman always wore a simple ostrich feather in her hair. In Egyptian, "to speak according to Maat" means to tell the truth.

the land of magic, there was a way for the dead to avoid this work. Small mummy statuettes, called *shabti,* were placed in the tomb of the dead to take care of the more tedious chores.

Religious beliefs vary among different peoples, and they evolve over the course of time. New beliefs mix with old ones, changing them and responding to the needs of different civilizations. And yet, much that is essential remains. The Egyptians, with their highly evolved manner of preparing for death, have left us valuable evidence about who they were and what they imagined, feared, and dreamed about in life.

The Devourer

According to The Books of the Dead, the Devourer ate those who behaved badly in life. With her crocodile head, her lion's chest, and the hindquarters of a hippopotamus, she was quite a frightening monster.

FIND OUT MORE

Bendick, Jeanne. *Egyptian Tombs*. New York: Franklin Watts, 1989.

Harris, Geraldine. *Ancient Egypt* (Cultural Atlas for Young People). New York: Facts on File, 1990.

Hart, George. *Ancient Egypt* (Eyewitness Books). New York: Alfred A. Knopf, 1990.

Macauley, David. *Pyramid*. New York: Houghton Mifflin Co., 1975.

Odijk, Pamela. *Egyptians*. Englewood Cliffs, New Jersey: Silver Burdett Press, 1989.

GLOSSARY

Amulet. Charm worn as magic protection against evil spirits.

Amun-Re. Principal god of Egypt in the New Kingdom.

Bastet. Daughter of Re; cat goddess of joy.

Book of the Dead. Scroll with prayers, spells, and instructions to guide people in the afterlife.

Chapel. Mortuary; small building where common people were buried.

Dynasty. Name for the period of time when rulers were related through family.

Embalmer. Person who preserves a body. *See* **Mummification**

Hathor. Goddess of love and protector of the dead.

Hieratic. Simplified writing in which drawings are reduced to dashes, strokes, and curves.

Hieroglyphic. Egyptian writing.

Horus. Son of Isis and Osiris who defeated his uncle Seth in battle and became ruler over Egypt.

Ideogram. *See* **Pictograph**

Isis. Osiris's wife and mother of Horus; goddess of maternal love.

Khnum. Ram-headed god who ruled over the dangerous Nile cataracts, or rapids.

Maat. Daughter of the sun god Re; goddess of justice and truth.

Mastaba. Flat-topped rectangular building where a king's relatives were buried.

Medou netcher. Egyptians' name for their writing.

Memphis. Capital of Egypt; seat of the pharaoh.

Mummification. Process of preserving and wrapping a dead body.

Mummy. Body of a dead person that has been both preserved through embalming and wrapped in linen.

Obelisk. Pillar with pointed tip carved with names of kings and words to the gods.

Osiris. God of vegetation and the underworld.

Papyrus. Reed native to Egypt from which paper was made.

Pharaoh. Name for Egyptian king meaning "great house," or palace of the king.

Phonogram. Symbol used to represent a sound.

Pictograph. Drawing used to represent objects.

Prophet. Priest whose job was to look after the temple in the name of the pharaoh.

Pylon. Gateway to a pyramid.

Pyramid. Massive tomb with triangular sides.

Re. Sun god; principal god of Egypt.

Scribe. Official writer for the king.

Seth. God of the desert; brother and murderer of Osiris.

Sphinx. Symbol of divine power with a lion's body and the head of a ram, a hawk, or a king or queen.

Temple. Religious building to house a god.

Thebes. Religious center of Egypt.

Thoth. God of the moon; patron of scribes and writing.

INDEX